PRAISE MY PET!

ADULT COLORING BOOK

WWW.PRAISEMYPET.COM

Color Sadie!

Color Gizmo!

Color Niko!

Color Yoshi!

Color Tinker Belle!

Color Baby Girl!

Color Ms. Belle!

Color Savannah and Bella!

Color Dakota!

Color Kilo, Ben, Misty and Sasha!

16

Color Zeus!

Color Fledge, Ace and Myles!

Color Harlee!

18

Color Hooch!

Color Baylee Gilly Ozzy!

Color Blanco and Frankie!

19

Color Copper, Storm and Whitley!

Color Max and Miley!

21

Color Turbo!

Color Bella, Polly and Angie!

23

Color Buddy Boy Tonders!

Color Nibbler and Shiloh!

25

Color Pepper and Jax!

Color Bleu!

Color Peanut!

Color Perry!

Color Olivia!

Color Gigi and Mia!

31

Color Boojie, Baxter, Izzy and Stella!

Color Dusty!

Color Bella!

Color Petey and Ms. Bootsie!

Color Tazzy, Chloe and Bootsy!

33

Color Chewbacca!

Color Kingston!

Color Bruno!

36

Color Boots!

Color Jasmine and Quayvo!

37

Color Monty and Boone!

Color Mayleigh!

Color Galletas!

41

Color Mione, Cato, Nera, Dante, Voodoo and Obi!

Color Milo!

44

Color Suka and Kanna!

45

Color Xena!

Color Nancy!

46

Color Glacier, Jolly and Princess!

49

Color Lizzie Belle and Simba Lee!

Color Chilli, Shelby and Nippsy!

51

Color Henry, Lulu and Ozzy!

52

Color Bruce and Ralphie!

Color Bella and Teddy!

Color Kaine!

Color Jetty Marie!

56

Color Kassie and Kenna!

Color Roxy!

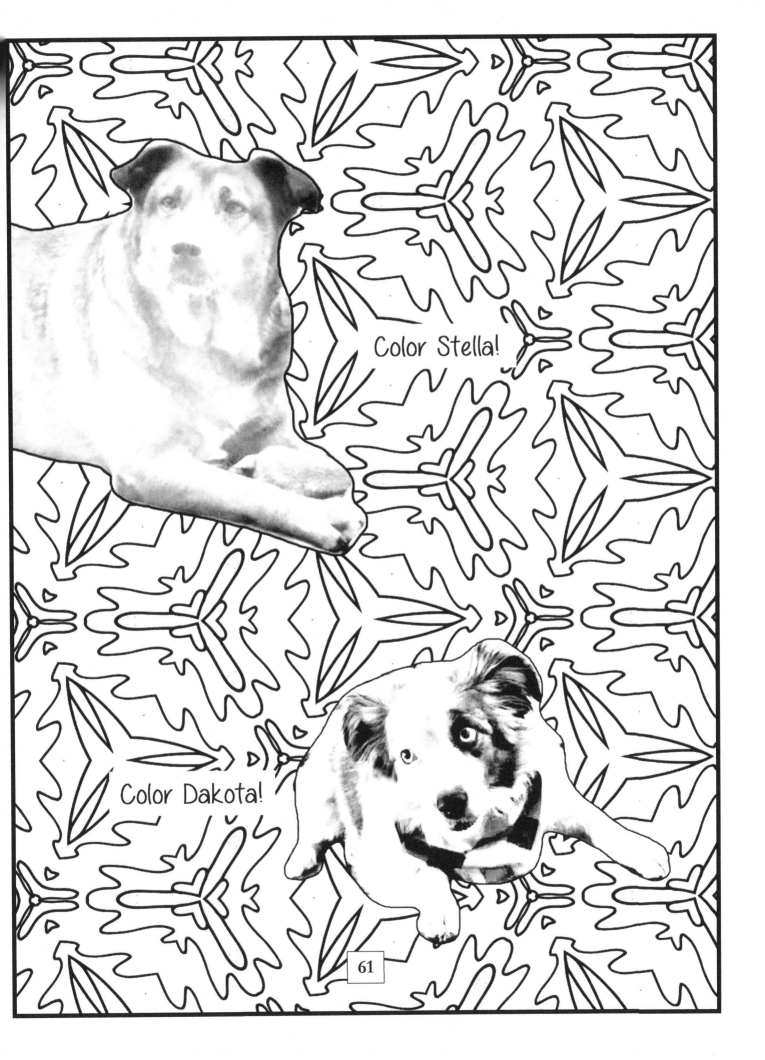

Color Sammy and Rusty!

Color Omar!

Color Crackers!

Color Mia Sofia Cali!

Color Niner and Pearl!

Color Six, Sullivan , Arya Daenerys, Wrenley Targaryen and Brann Wylis!

Color Comet!

Color Tallie and Georgia!

Color Harley!

Color Isabella and Dixie!

Color Lakin, Koda and Carson!

81

Color Isabelle!

Color Shark and Honey!

Color Sunnie!

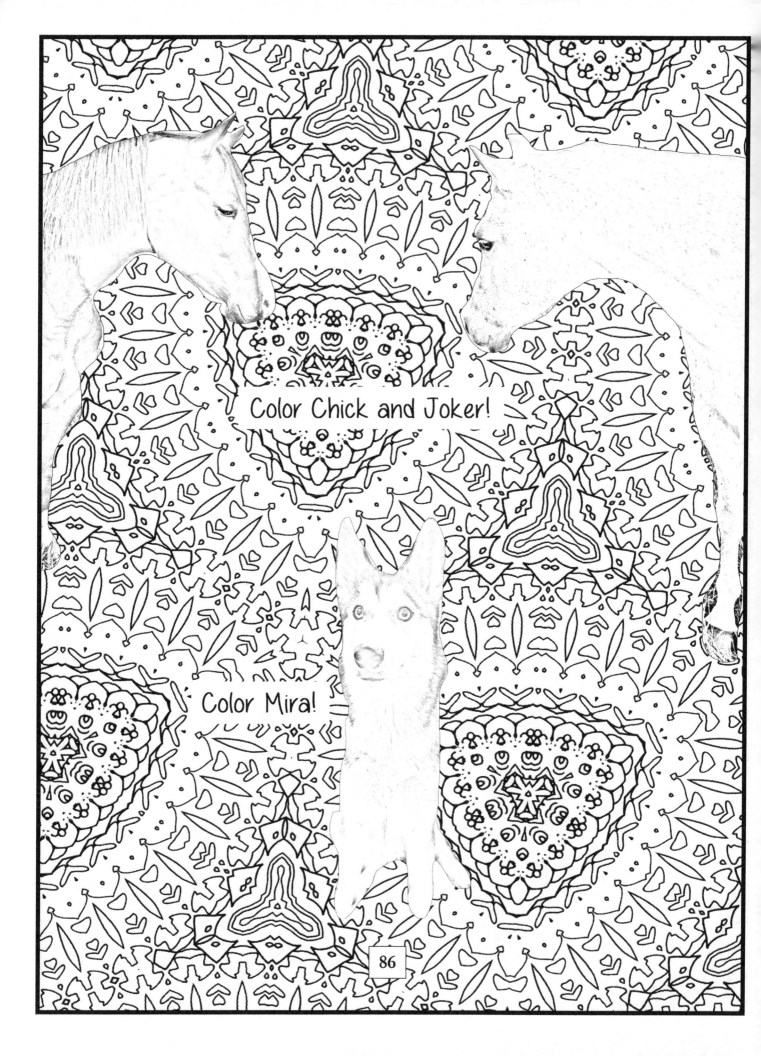

Color Chick and Joker!

Color Mira!

86

Color Lilo and Radio!

Color Tweek and Misty!

Color Marnie and Luci!

Color Oliver!

Color Dude!

Color Taco Belle!

93

Color Finley!

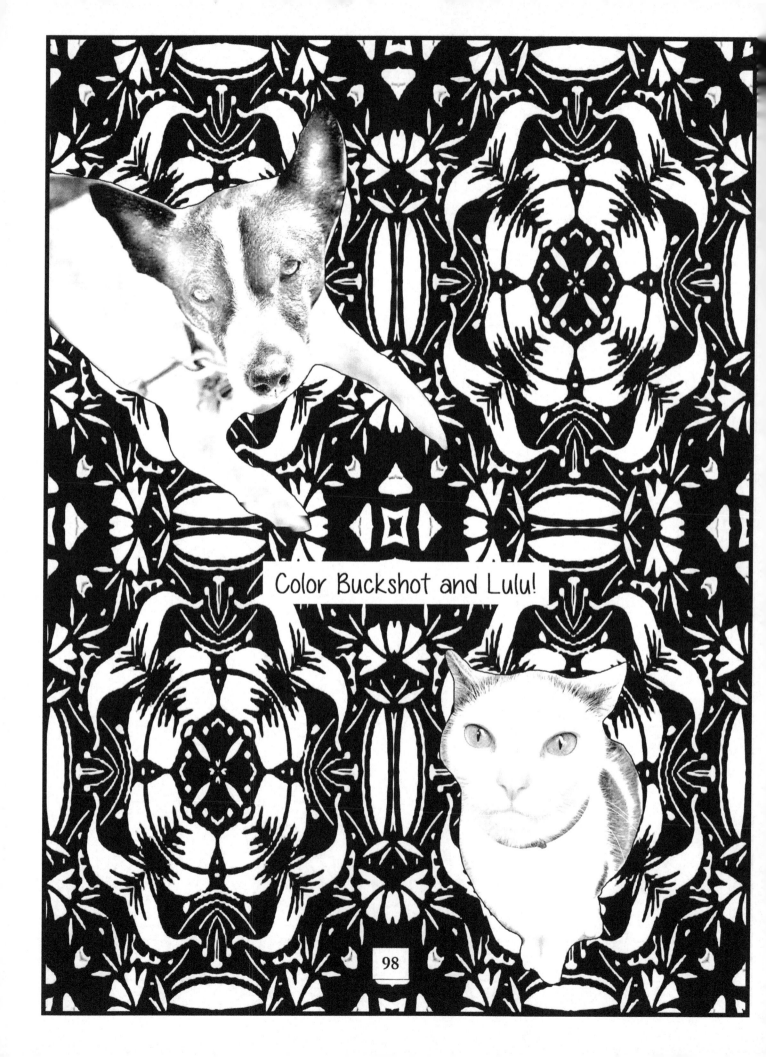

Color Buckshot and Lulu!

98

Color Zo and Max!

Color Koga!

Color Karley and Lucy!

We hope you enjoyed our coloring book! If you'd like to see YOUR pet in one of our upcoming coloring books, visit www.praisemypet.com/pages/send-us-your-pet-photos

Happy coloring!

59368618R00057